Embracing Calm

Nora Sage's Guide to Stress Management and Positive Living

Techniques, Tools, and Insights for a Balanced Life

By Nora Sage

No part of this publication may be reproduced, distributed, or transmitted in any form or by any means, including photocopying, recording, or other electronic or mechanical methods, without the prior written permission of the publisher, except in the case of brief quotations embodied in critical reviews and certain other noncommercial uses permitted by copyright law. For permission requests, write to the publisher at the address below.

E-Volve Books
Pawleys Island, SC 29585

Disclaimer

The information provided in this book, ***Embracing Calm: Nora Sage's Guide to Stress Management and Positive Living,*** is for general informational and educational purposes only. The author and publisher of this book make no representation or warranties concerning the accuracy, applicability, fitness, or completeness of the contents of this book.

The information contained within this book should not be used as a substitute for professional medical advice, diagnosis, or treatment. Always consult with a qualified healthcare professional before beginning any diet, exercise, or stress management program.

The author and publisher shall not be liable for any loss, injury, or damage allegedly arising from any information or suggestion in this book.

Introduction

STRESS: THE SILENT JUGGERNAUT OF MODERN LIFE

Welcome to the rollercoaster of modern life, where stress is the uninvited guest who just loves to crash the party! Picture stress as that sneaky ninja, lurking in the shadows of our daily hustle, ready to pounce when we least expect it. It's like that extra spice in our life's dish - sometimes it adds flavor, but too much, and whoa, it's a recipe for disaster!

So, what's this buzz about stress? Let's break it down without the mumbo-jumbo. Imagine stress as your body's alarm system. It's like your internal siren that blares out when you're running late for a meeting, juggling bills, or dealing with that never-ending family drama. It's your body's way of saying, "Hey, gear up, we've got a situation!"

But here's the twist - our lives today are like being on a never-ending treadmill of these 'situations.' We're constantly bombarded with emails, social media notifications, and the pressure to be our best selves. It's like being in a never-ending game of whack-a-mole, but instead of moles, it's emails, deadlines, and social commitments.

This non-stop action adventure isn't just a wild ride; it's leaving its mark. When stress becomes your unwanted BFF, it can lead to sleepless nights, a tummy in knots, and feeling like you're always running on fumes. It's like carrying an invisible backpack filled with bricks - it weighs you down, and you don't even realize it!

But fear not! This book isn't about doom and gloom. It's your secret playbook to outsmart stress. Think of it as your guide to turning down the volume of life's chaos. We're going to dive into the world of stress like detectives, uncover its sneaky hiding spots, and equip you with an arsenal of stress-busting moves.

So, buckle up, my friend! You're about to embark on a vibrant journey to reclaim your peace, find your zen, and give stress the boot. Let's turn that stress mess into a stress-less success!

MY DANCE WITH THE STRESS MONSTER

Hey there, fellow life jugglers! Let me tell you about my tango with the stress monster. Picture this: I'm a middle-aged dynamo, a mom, a wife, and your go-to guru for all things fitness. My life's like a circus, and I'm the ringmaster, trying to keep the lions, tightrope walkers, and clowns in check.

So, there I was, a typical Tuesday (or was it Wednesday? Who knows, they all blur together!). The alarm clock was my starter pistol - off to the races! Lunches to pack, emails screaming for attention, and oh, the joys of finding that elusive matching sock for my youngest. Add to that, my daily rendezvous with the treadmill, because hey, fitness is my jam!

But then, the plot thickens. Picture me, dashing around like a contestant on a game show where the prize is just making it through the day without a meltdown. There's the PTA meeting I almost forgot (yikes!), the grocery run (because apparently, we need food), and let's not forget playing peacekeeper between my kids and their never-ending bickering.

It hit me one evening, right in the middle of my 'famous' (or infamous, depending on who you ask) spaghetti and meatballs. I'm twirling pasta, and suddenly, my heart's racing, my breath's short, and the room feels like it's closing in. Hello, stress-induced panic attack, nice of you to drop by unannounced!

That was my wake-up call, folks. I realized I was trying to sprint through a marathon. I was the fitness pro who preached wellness but was letting stress do the cha-cha on my well-being. Irony much?

This was my moment of truth. I had to walk the talk, not just for me but for my family, my clients, and hey, for every superwoman out there trying to do it all. It was time to rewrite the script, change the dance steps with stress, and maybe, just maybe, find a way to make it do a little jig to my tune instead.

So, grab your popcorn, and let's dive into this adventure. I'm about to spill the beans on how I turned my stress mess into a groove of wellness and balance. And guess what? If I can do it, so can you!

WHAT'S IN STORE FOR YOU IN THIS STRESS-BUSTING SAGA

Alright, my fabulous stress-busting comrades, here's the scoop on what this no-nonsense, kick-stress-in-the-butt guide has in store for you. Think of this book as your personal stress whisperer, your secret weapon in the battle against the chaos of everyday life.

1. Stress Decoded: First up, we're going to unravel the mystery of stress. It's like getting the inside gossip on the biggest drama queen of your life - stress itself! We'll peek behind the curtain to understand what makes stress tick and why it loves to crash our peace party.

2. Your Stress Detective Kit: Next, we're turning you into a stress detective. You'll learn how to spot the sneaky signs of stress that try to go incognito. It's like having X-ray vision for your soul - nothing gets past you!

3. The Stress-Busting Toolbox: Then, it's time to arm you with an arsenal of stress-busting tools. We're talking easy-peasy techniques that you can slip into your day faster than you can say 'latte, please!' From breathing tricks that calm you quicker than a catnap to mindset shifts that are like a spa day for your brain - we've got you covered.

4. Lifestyle Overhaul: But wait, there's more! We're going to jazz up your lifestyle to make it a stress-proof fortress. Imagine transforming your daily grind into a daily groove. We'll tweak those little habits that add up to big changes. It's like a makeover for your routine, but way more fun.

5. Real Talk with Real Experts: And because we're all about keeping it real, you'll hear from the pros - psychologists, wellness gurus, and folks who've danced with stress and stepped on its toes. They're spilling their secrets, and trust me, it's juicy stuff.

6. Your Personal Stress-Busting Plan: Finally, we're crafting your personalized stress-busting plan. It's like a tailor-made outfit, but for your mental well-being. We're talking custom-fit strategies that work for your unique, fabulous life.

So, are you ready to turn the tables on stress? To make it your dance partner instead of the party crasher? Let's embark on this journey of transformation, laughter, and a whole lot of 'aha!' moments. By the end of this book, you won't just be managing stress; you'll be showing it the door with style and a sassy smile.

Chapter 1
Understanding Stress

STRESS: THE UNSEEN PARTY CRASHER IN YOUR BODY'S BASH

Welcome to the first stop on our stress-busting journey! Here, we're going to get up close and personal with stress. Think of it as meeting the mysterious stranger who's been crashing at your body's party uninvited. It's time to put a face to the name!

Stress, Unmasked: What Exactly Is It?

Picture stress as your body's built-in alarm system. It's like your internal bodyguard, jumping into action when it senses trouble. Whether it's running late for a meeting or dealing with a mountain of bills, stress is your body's way of saying, "Hey, gear up, we've got dragons to slay!"

The Biology of Stress: Your Body's Behind-the-Scenes Drama

Now, let's dive into the behind-the-scenes action. When stress enters the scene, your body goes all Hollywood "action movie" on you. It releases these little chemical messengers, like adrenaline and cortisol, which are like your body's own version of a superhero squad. They get your heart pumping faster, make your breath quicken, and sharpen your senses - it's like getting ready to run a sprint or lift a car (okay, maybe not a car, but you get the idea).

Stress: The Good, The Bad, The Ugly

Here's the kicker: stress isn't all villainous. Sometimes, it's the hero of the hour. That burst of energy when you're dodging a frisbee or nailing a presentation? That's stress, giving you a high-five. But when stress decides to move in and take a permanent spot on your couch, that's when things get messy. Chronic stress is like having an overzealous bodyguard who doesn't know when to chill. It can lead to all sorts of health shenanigans - none of which are the fun kind.

In this chapter, we're setting the stage to understand stress in all its glory - the good, the bad, and the downright annoying. We're keeping it light, a bit cheeky, but totally informative. Stay tuned, because we're about to turn you into a stress-busting ninja!

STRESS: THE QUICK FLING VS. THE BAD ROMANCE

Alright, let's roll up our sleeves and dive into the world of stress types. Think of stress as coming in two main flavors: Acute and Chronic. It's like comparing a whirlwind weekend adventure to a never-ending soap opera. Let's break it down:

Acute Stress: The Flash in the Pan

Picture acute stress as that adrenaline-pumping moment when you narrowly avoid a fender bender, or you're about to give the performance of your life on stage. It's short, sharp, and intense - like a shot of espresso to your system. Your heart races, your palms get sweaty, but hey, it's over as quickly as it started. This kind of stress is like a guest star in the sitcom of your life - pops in, stirs things up, and then exits stage left.

Chronic Stress: The Unwanted Roommate

Now, let's talk about chronic stress. This one's the sneaky, lingering kind. Imagine a drip, drip, drip of stress that just doesn't let up - like juggling work deadlines, while managing home life, and trying to remember if you fed the cat. It's the stress that feels like it's moved in, unpacked its bags, and decided to stay awhile. Chronic stress is like that annoying roommate who eats your food, messes up your space, and just won't leave. It's the kind that can start to mess with your health, mood, and overall zest for life.

Understanding these two tango partners of stress is key. Acute stress can be a bit of a thrill, a momentary challenge that we overcome. But chronic stress? That's the one we need to show the door. So, stick with me, and let's get ready to kick some chronic stress butt and turn our lives into a stress-free fiesta!

Now, let's chat about the party crashers of our life stages - those common stress triggers that seem to follow us like a shadow, no matter our age or phase of life. Stress doesn't discriminate; it's an equal-opportunity annoyer. But, the reasons we get stressed? Ah, those change with the seasons of our lives. Let's take a whirlwind tour through these stages and their stress sidekicks:

The Roaring 20s: Young, Wild, and Stressed

Picture your 20s as that rollercoaster you can't wait to ride but then scream all the way through. It's all about finding your feet - college deadlines, the first 'real' job, and the dating scene that's more confusing than a Sudoku puzzle. It's like juggling flaming torches while riding a unicycle.

The Thriving 30s: Adulting is Hard

Welcome to the 30s, where 'adulting' becomes a reality, not just a trendy hashtag. Career pressures, maybe starting a family, or buying that first home that comes with a mortgage that feels like a mountain. It's like playing a game of Tetris where the blocks just. Keep. Coming.

The Fabulous 40s: Midlife's Juggling Act

Ah, the 40s - the age of questioning, "Am I doing this right?" It's a juggling act between career peaks (or pits), growing kids (who suddenly know everything), and maybe caring for aging parents. It's like being a circus performer, but you never trained for this.

The Feisty 50s and Beyond: The Renaissance Years

Now, the 50s and beyond, that's where life throws curveballs and bouquets. Maybe it's dealing with an empty nest, thinking about retirement (yikes!), or rediscovering passions and hobbies. It's like opening a mystery box each day - surprise!

In every stage, stress has its favorite hiding spots. But here's the good news - no matter the stage, the tools in this book are like your stress-busting Swiss army knife. Ready to slice through the stress of your roaring 20s, navigate the adulting of your 30s, balance the 40s circus, and savor the renaissance of your 50s and beyond. Let's turn each stage into a stress-conquering victory lap!

STRESS: THE BODY AND MIND TANGO

Alright, let's talk about what happens when stress decides to tango with our bodies and minds. It's like having an untrained dance partner - sometimes you get stepped on!

The Mind Games of Stress

Imagine your brain on stress. It's like having a browser with too many tabs open - everything slows down, and good luck finding that one tab you need! Stress can make you feel like you're in a mental fog, where making decisions is as hard as solving a Rubik's Cube blindfolded. It can turn your mood into a yo-yo - one minute you're up, the next you're down. And anxiety? That's stress's favorite dance move. It's like having an inner alarm that just won't quit.

The Body Boogie with Stress

Now, let's shimmy over to what stress does to the body. Ever felt your heart racing like it's trying to win a marathon, all because you're stressed? That's your body doing the stress samba. And let's not forget the muscle tension - it's like your body's trying to turn into a human pretzel. Stress can also crash your sleep party, leaving you tossing and turning like a salad. And when it comes to eating - stress can either make you lose your appetite or turn you into a snack monster.

But here's the kicker - while stress can lead us on this wild dance, we're not just passive wallflowers. We've got moves of our own. And in this book, I'm going to show you how to outdance stress, whether it's messing with your mind or boogying with your body. So, lace up your dancing shoes, and let's get ready to rumba!

Chapter 2
The Science Behind Stress

Welcome to the lab of life, where we're about to play detective and uncover the secrets of stress. Think of this chapter as your backstage pass to the science concert of stress. We're not just skimming the surface; we're diving deep - but in a fun, "I totally get this" kind of way. No lab coats or jargon here, just spicy, punchy truths about what's really going on when stress enters the stage.

The Brain-Body Stress Dance

First up, we're exploring how stress gets your brain and body to tango - sometimes a bit too intensely. It's like discovering why your inner orchestra sometimes plays rock music instead of a soothing symphony.

Hormones: The Body's Stress DJs

Next, we'll spin the decks with stress hormones like cortisol, the body's own resident DJ, pumping out beats that get everything moving - sometimes a little too fast. It's like having a nightclub in your body, and cortisol's in charge of the tunes.

When Stress Overstays Its Welcome

Then, we're talking about what happens when stress decides to throw a never-ending party in your life. Spoiler alert: it's not the kind of party you want to be at. We'll look at the long-term party fouls of unmanaged stress.

Stress: The Social Butterfly of Health Conditions

And finally, we'll see how stress loves to mingle and mix with other health conditions. It's like the social butterfly that connects with various aspects of your health, sometimes stirring up trouble.

So, are you ready to become a stress scientist? To peek behind the curtain and understand the wizardry of stress? Let's turn those question marks into exclamation points and master the art of stress-busting!

THE SCIENCE BEHIND STRESS

STRESS: THE BRAIN-BODY ROLLERCOASTER RIDE

Hop on, folks! We're about to take a wild ride into how stress throws a party in your brain and body – and trust me, it's a bash that can turn bashful!

The Brain Under Siege

- Imagine your brain as the command center of a high-tech spaceship. When stress hits, it's like an asteroid field suddenly appearing on the radar. Your brain goes into red alert, sending signals all over the ship. You might feel your thoughts racing like a sports car at full throttle, or find it hard to focus, like trying to read a book in a disco. This is your brain on stress - it's busy, buzzy, and a bit bonkers!

The Body's Boogie with Stress

Now, let's shimmy down to your body. When your brain is doing the stress tango, it sends signals to your body to join the dance. Your heart starts beating like it's drumming for a rock band, your muscles tense up like they're prepping for a weightlifting contest, and your breath quickens like you're blowing up a hundred balloons. It's your body's way of prepping for action - whether there's a real emergency or it's just your boss asking for those reports.

Stress: The Unseen Choreographer

Here's the thing - stress is like an invisible choreographer, directing the moves of your brain and body. Sometimes, it's a helpful coach, getting you ready to leap into action. But other times, it's like a drill sergeant, pushing you too hard, too fast. And let's be real, nobody likes a bossy choreographer!

Understanding how stress affects our brain and body is like getting a backstage pass to the biggest show of our lives. It helps us spot when stress is turning from a helpful stagehand into a pushy director. So, let's learn how to take the lead in this dance, shall we?

Stay tuned, because we're about to turn this stress dance into a stress-busting prance!

THE SCIENCE BEHIND STRESS

Cortisol: The DJ of the Stress Party

Alright, let's zoom in on cortisol, the headliner in the stress hormone music festival. Think of cortisol as the DJ spinning the decks in your body's nightclub. When it's just the right amount of tunes, the vibe is fantastic. But when the music's too loud for too long, well, that's when the party gets out of hand.

Cortisol: The Body's Alarm Bell

Imagine cortisol as your body's built-in alarm system. It's like the friend who gives you a nudge when you're dozing off in a meeting. When you're stressed, cortisol wakes up your body with a jolt of energy. It's like downing an espresso shot when you need that extra zing. This is great for those 'fight or flight' moments - like dodging a runaway shopping cart in the grocery store parking lot.

The Ups and Downs of the Cortisol Coaster

But here's the twist: cortisol is a bit of a drama queen. It loves to keep the party going, even when it's time to wind down. If your body is constantly pumping out cortisol, it's like having a non-stop rave in your system. You might feel wired, tired, and everything in between. It's like riding a rollercoaster that doesn't know how to stop.

When the Party Doesn't Stop: Too Much Cortisol

Too much cortisol can crash your health party. It can mess with your sleep, make you crave all the sugary snacks, and even play tricks on your memory (ever walked into a room and forgot why?). It's like having a DJ that doesn't know when to turn down the volume.

So, what's the takeaway? Understanding cortisol's role in stress is like knowing how to work the soundboard at a party. You want the tunes, but you don't want them to drown out everything else. In the upcoming sections, we'll explore how to be the master of your cortisol levels, turning you into the DJ of your own stress party! Let's get ready to remix our stress response and turn down the cortisol chaos!

THE SCIENCE BEHIND STRESS

When Stress Overstays Its Welcome: The Long-Term House Party

Imagine stress as that guest who came for a weekend bash and then decided to crash on your couch indefinitely.

At first, it was all fun and games, but now the dishes are piling up, and your once peaceful home feels like a 24/7 discotheque. That's what unmanaged stress is like - it starts as a temporary hustle and bustle but can turn your life into a never-ending, not-so-fun fiesta.

The Never-Ending Stress Marathon

When stress becomes your permanent roommate, it's like being stuck on a treadmill that's always speeding up. You're running and running, but the 'off' button seems broken. This non-stop stress marathon can leave you feeling exhausted, yet somehow, you're still lying awake at 3 AM, counting the sheep that just won't jump the fence.

The Domino Effect on Your Health

Unchecked stress doesn't just tap dance on your nerves; it can start a domino effect on your health. It's like a party where one broken vase leads to a food fight, which leads to a full-blown house trashing. Chronic stress can lead to a buffet of not-so-great things like high blood pressure, a tummy that's always in knots, and a sugar craving that just won't quit. It's like your body is constantly in a state of red alert, and after a while, the alarms just start to wear you out.

The Mood Rollercoaster

And let's not forget the emotional rollercoaster. Long-term stress can make your mood jump around like a ping-pong ball. One minute you're up, the next you're down, and sometimes you're just flat-out irritable - like a bear woken up from hibernation. It's hard to enjoy the party when your emotions are doing the cha-cha without your permission.

But here's the good news: this book is your guide to showing unmanaged stress the door. We're about to learn how to turn down the volume of life's party and bring back the zen.

So, get ready to reclaim your space, find your peace, and send that long-term stress packing. It's time to turn your home back into a haven, not a 24/7 stress nightclub!

THE SCIENCE BEHIND STRESS

Stress: The Not-So-Silent Health Party Crasher

Alright, let's chat about how stress, the ultimate party crasher, loves to mingle with other health conditions. It's like that guest who not only overstays their welcome but also invites friends over without asking. Stress doesn't just hang out solo; it often brings along a crew of other health issues, turning your body into a crowded, chaotic dance floor.

Stress and the Heart: A Troublesome Tango

First up, let's shimmy over to your heart. Stress and heart health are like dance partners in a tango - a bit too intense and not always in a good way. Chronic stress can make your heart work overtime, like it's running a marathon every day. This can lead to high blood pressure and other heart-related shenanigans. It's like your heart is constantly dancing to a fast-paced beat, and not the fun kind.

Stress and the Tummy: The Digestive Disco

Next, let's boogie down to your belly. Stress loves to throw a disco in your digestive system. Ever had butterflies in your stomach before a big event? That's stress doing the cha-cha. But when stress decides to throw a rave in your gut, it can lead to things like heartburn, indigestion, or even irritable bowel syndrome (IBS). It's like your digestive system is partying a little too hard, and not in a good way.

Stress and the Sugar Swing

Now, let's swing over to blood sugar. Stress can make your blood sugar levels swing like they're in a jazz band. For those managing conditions like diabetes, this can be like trying to dance on a tightrope. Stress makes managing blood sugar levels a bit more like a juggling act - and who needs that extra performance pressure?

Stress and the Immune System: The Undercover Party Pooper

And don't forget the immune system. When stress throws a party, your immune system can start to slack off, like a bouncer taking a nap. This means you might catch colds or other infections more easily. It's like stress is sneaking in unwanted party crashers (germs) while your immune system's guard is down.

So, what's the takeaway from this health party? Knowing how stress interacts with different aspects of our health is like having a roadmap to navigate a crowded party. It helps us spot where stress might be causing a ruckus and how to calm things down.

Stay tuned, because we're about to learn how to be the best health party hosts and keep stress from turning our bodies into a wild bash!

Chapter 3
Identifying Your Stress Triggers

Welcome to Chapter 3, where we turn into stress detectives, armed with magnifying glasses and a dash of sass. It's time to play a game of 'Whodunnit?' with our stress. This chapter is all about uncovering those sneaky stress triggers that like to play hide-and-seek in our daily lives. Think of it as a treasure hunt, but instead of looking for gold, we're hunting down what turns our chill day into a thrill ride (and not the fun kind).

Spotting the Stress Bandits

We'll start by learning how to spot those pesky stress bandits. Is it the morning traffic? The never-ending notifications on your phone? Or maybe it's that overflowing laundry basket that's giving you the side-eye. We're going to identify these culprits with the precision of a cat spotting a laser pointer.

The Mirror of Self-Awareness

Next, we'll dive into the sparkling pool of self-awareness. It's like holding up a mirror to your life and seeing where stress likes to photobomb your peace. Understanding your reactions and emotions is like having a secret decoder ring that reveals the hidden messages behind your stress.

Your Stress Journal: The Diary of a Stress Detective

And here's the fun part - you'll start your very own Stress Journal. It's not just any diary; it's your personal logbook for tracking the who, what, when, and why of your stress. Think of it as your daily debrief, like a detective jotting down clues after a day on the case.

By the end of this chapter, you'll be a pro at pinpointing your stress triggers. You'll know them like the back of your hand, ready to catch them red-handed before they can throw confetti on your parade.

So, grab your detective hat and let's start this stress-sleuthing adventure!

IDENTIFYING YOUR STRESS TRIGGERS

Playing Detective: Spotting Those Sneaky Stressors

Alright, fellow stress sleuths, let's dive into the art of spotting those sneaky stressors. It's like being a detective in a mystery movie, where the clues are hidden in plain sight. We're going to uncover these hidden culprits with flair and a bit of fun.

The Art of Stress Spotting

Think of your day as a puzzle. Each piece, whether it's rushing to meet a deadline or dealing with a temper tantrum from your toddler, can be a potential stressor. We're going to learn how to look at these pieces with a magnifying glass. Is it the traffic jam that sets your teeth on edge? Or maybe it's the mountain of dishes in the sink? We'll identify these moments, big or small, that crank up your stress levels.

Stressor Spotting Signs

Your body and mind often send out flares when stress is on the rise. Maybe your heart starts to race like it's in the Grand Prix, or your stomach ties itself into knots. Perhaps you get snappy like a crab or feel as drained as a smartphone battery at 1%. These are your body's ways of waving a red flag, saying, "Hey, something's up!"

The Power of Patterns

As we play detective, we'll start to see patterns. Like, do you turn into a stress-monster every Monday morning? Or does your mood plummet when you're scrolling through social media? Spotting these patterns is like cracking a secret code - it gives you the power to anticipate and prepare for these stressors before they jump out and say 'boo!'

By the end of this section, you'll be a pro at recognizing your personal stressors. It's like having a stress radar that beeps whenever a stressor is near. With this superpower, you'll be ready to tackle these stressors head-on, turning them from scary monsters into manageable mice. Let's keep our detective hats on and continue this thrilling stress-busting adventure!

The Self-Awareness Superpower: Tuning Into Your Stress Signals

Welcome to the world of self-awareness, where you're the star of your own show, and stress is just a pesky supporting character trying to steal the spotlight. It's time to tune into your inner frequencies and turn self-awareness into your superpower for managing stress.

The Inner Mirror: Reflecting on Reactions

Imagine self-awareness as a mirror that reflects not just your face, but your thoughts, feelings, and reactions. It's like having a personal coach inside your head, giving you the play-by-play on how you react to stress. Do you bite your nails when deadlines loom? Do you snap like a twig when the kids leave toys everywhere? This inner mirror helps you see these patterns, clear as day.

Emotional Check-Ins: The Daily Debrief

Let's make emotional check-ins a part of your daily routine, like brushing your teeth or scrolling through your social feeds. It's like taking a moment to interview yourself: "How am I feeling right now? Am I as frazzled as a blender on high speed, or as cool as a cucumber?" These check-ins are your secret weapon in understanding and managing your stress.

The Power of Pause: Slowing Down the Stress Train

In the fast-paced movie of life, self-awareness is your pause button. It gives you a moment to breathe, step back, and look at your stressors from the balcony, not just the dance floor. When you're about to react to stress, hit that pause button. Take a deep breath. It's like slowing down a fast-forward video to normal speed, giving you the clarity to choose how you want to respond, not just react.

By embracing self-awareness, you're not just managing stress; you're choreographing a graceful dance with it. You're in control, leading the steps, and turning potential missteps into elegant twirls. So, let's keep this self-awareness party going and turn stress management into a rhythm we can all groove to!

IDENTIFYING YOUR STRESS TRIGGERS

The Stress Journal: Your Daily Dose of Detective Work

Now, let's talk about your new sidekick in this stress-busting adventure - the Stress Journal. Think of it as your personal diary, but instead of secrets and crushes, it's all about tracking those sneaky stress gremlins. It's your daily logbook, your stress detective's notebook, where you jot down the who, what, when, and why of your stress episodes.

Setting Up Your Stress Journal

Grab a notebook, a pen, and your Sherlock Holmes hat - it's time to get started. Your stress journal can be as simple or fancy as you like. A plain notebook? Perfect. An app on your phone? Fabulous. The key is to make it easy and fun. Decorate it, name it, make it your stress-busting buddy.

Daily Entries: The Stress Chronicles

Each day, take a few minutes to write in your journal. Had a moment where you felt like a kettle about to whistle? Jot it down. Noticed your heart doing the samba during a meeting? Write it out. It's like being a reporter on the front lines of your life, capturing the big and small moments of stress.

Spotting Patterns: Connecting the Dots

- After a while, you'll start to see patterns. Maybe you're more stressed on Mondays or when you skip your morning jog. It's like connecting the dots in a constellation, forming a picture of your stress landscape. These insights are gold - they're your clues to managing stress better.

Reflect and React: Turning Insights into Action

The real magic happens when you use these insights to make changes. Found out that traffic jams turn you into a stress monster? Maybe it's time to try a new route or a podcast to keep you company. Realized that too much caffeine makes you jittery? Perhaps switch to herbal tea after lunch. Your journal entries are not just observations; they're stepping stones to a more stress-free you.

Keeping a stress journal is like having a conversation with yourself about what makes you tick and what ticks you off. It's your personal roadmap to navigating the bumpy roads of life with a bit more ease and a lot more joy. So, let's start journaling and turn those stress scribbles into a masterpiece of calm!

Chapter 4
Proven Techniques to Manage Stress

Welcome to Chapter 4, the treasure trove of stress-busting secrets! This is where we roll up our sleeves and dive into the fun, practical stuff. Think of this chapter as your personal stress-relief workshop, filled with tools, tips, and tricks to turn you into a zen master. We're talking real-deal techniques that are like having a 'chill pill' for every stress-filled moment.

Breathe Easy: The Magic of Deep Breathing

First, we'll explore the superpower of deep breathing. It's like having a secret weapon in your back pocket. Feeling like a balloon ready to pop? We'll show you how a few deep breaths can transform you from a stress ball to a serene swan. It's simple, it's quick, and boy, does it work wonders!

Mindfulness and Meditation: Your Mental Chill Zone

Next, we'll step into the world of mindfulness and meditation. Imagine having a mental escape room where stress can't find you. We'll guide you through easy-peasy techniques to quiet the mind chatter and find your inner peace. It's like giving your brain a mini-vacation.

Get Moving: Shake Off the Stress

Time to get physical! We'll jump into how physical activity can be your dance partner in the tango against stress. Whether it's a brisk walk, a yoga session, or a living room dance party, we'll show you how moving your body can shake off the stress. It's like hitting the refresh button on your mood.

Sleep: Your Nighttime Stress-Buster

And let's not forget the power of good ol' sleep. We'll dive into why catching those Z's is like giving your body and mind a nightly reboot. You'll learn tips to turn your bedroom into a stress-free sanctuary, ensuring you wake up feeling like a superhero ready to take on the world.

By the end of this chapter, you'll have a toolkit brimming with stress-busting techniques. You'll be ready to face stress head-on, with a smile on your face and some cool moves up your sleeve. So, let's get ready to kick stress to the curb and dance our way to serenity!

PROVEN TECHNIQUES TO MANAGE STRESS

Deep Breathing: The Stress-Busting Superhero in Your Lungs

Let's dive into the world of deep breathing, the unsung hero in our stress-busting toolkit. It's like discovering a secret superpower you never knew you had - hidden right under your nose (literally)!

The Magic of a Deep Breath

Imagine each deep breath as a mini stress-buster, working its magic every time you inhale and exhale. It's like hitting the pause button on life's crazy remote control. When you take a deep breath, it's not just air you're pulling in; it's like you're inflating a balloon of calm inside you, pushing out the stress as you exhale. It's a simple trick, but boy, does it pack a punch!

The How-To of Deep Breathing

Here's how you do it: Find a comfy spot. Sit down, stand up, or even lie down - whatever floats your boat. Now, take a slow, deep breath in, like you're smelling your favorite pizza. Feel your chest and belly rise - that's your body saying 'thank you' for the extra oxygen. Hold it for a second. Now, exhale like you're blowing out birthday candles - slow and steady. Repeat this a few times and voilà - you're on your way to being as cool as a cucumber.

The Benefits: Why Deep Breathing Rocks

Deep breathing is like a Swiss Army knife for your health. It helps lower your heart rate, making you feel as chill as a lounge chair by the beach. It reduces tension - goodbye, shoulder knots and hello, relaxation! It can even help clear your mind, making it easier to focus than a laser beam. And the best part? You can do it anywhere - in line at the grocery store, under your desk at work, or even while stuck in traffic. It's like having a stress relief button, always at your fingertips.

By mastering deep breathing, you're not just managing stress; you're telling it to take a hike. It's a tool that's always with you, no batteries required, no subscription needed. So, let's breathe our way to a stress-free life, one deep, relaxing breath at a time. Ready, set, inhale... and exhale!

PROVEN TECHNIQUES TO MANAGE STRESS

Mindfulness and Meditation: Your Brain's Spa Day

Welcome to the fabulous world of mindfulness and meditation, where your mind gets to kick back, relax, and sip on a cocktail of calm. This isn't just some fancy fad - it's like giving your brain a spa day, every day.

Mindfulness: The Art of Living in the Now

Picture mindfulness as the art of being the ultimate 'here and now' ninja. It's about being present in the moment, not lost in yesterday's regrets or tomorrow's worries. Imagine savoring your morning coffee, feeling the warmth of the cup, the aroma, the taste - that's mindfulness. It's like turning off the autopilot and really experiencing life as it happens. No more missing the beauty of now because you're stuck in the traffic jam of your thoughts.

Meditation: Your Mental Workout

Now, let's talk meditation. If mindfulness is about being present, meditation is like doing reps at the gym, but for your mind. It's about sitting down, closing your eyes, and giving your thoughts a time-out. You don't need incense or chanting; just you, a comfy spot, and a few minutes. It's like hitting the 'mute' button on the world's noise, letting your mind chill out and recharge.

The Benefits: Why They're Awesome

The perks of mindfulness and meditation? Oh, they're like the gift that keeps on giving. Stress reduction? Check. Improved focus? You bet. A sense of peace and well-being? Absolutely. It's like your mind is doing yoga, becoming more flexible and less prone to getting bent out of shape by life's twists and turns.

Making It a Habit: Your Daily Dose of Zen

The best part? You can weave mindfulness and meditation into your daily routine. A few minutes of meditation in the morning can set the tone for a calmer day. Mindful moments - like really listening to a friend or feeling the sun on your face - can be sprinkled throughout your day like little stress-busting confetti.

So, let's embrace mindfulness and meditation as our daily mental health vitamins. They're the secret sauce to keeping our cool in the kitchen of life. Ready to give your mind the TLC it deserves?

Let's dive into the zen zone!

Get Moving: The Stress-Busting Power of Physical Activity

Strap on your sneakers, folks - it's time to talk about physical activity, the ultimate stress-busting ally.

Think of it as your body's natural way of kicking stress in the behind. It's not just about getting fit; it's about flipping the off switch on stress.

Sweat It Out: The Stress Meltdown

When you get moving, it's like you're telling stress, "You're not the boss of me!" Whether it's a brisk walk, a funky dance session in your living room, or a full-on workout, physical activity gets those feel-good hormones (hello, endorphins!) pumping. It's like throwing a one-person dance party where stress isn't invited. You're sweating out the tension, and with every drop, you're washing away the worries.

The Variety Spice: Pick Your Flavor

The best part? There's no one-size-fits-all. Hate running? No problem. How about a bike ride, a swim, or even a vigorous round of vacuuming (yes, house chores count too!). It's all about finding your groove. Love to dance? Crank up the tunes and shake it out. Prefer quiet and calm? Yoga might be your stress-busting soulmate. The key is to find something you enjoy, so it feels less like a chore and more like a treat.

The Sneaky Stress-Buster: Everyday Moves

And hey, who said you need a gym membership? Take the stairs instead of the elevator, have a walking meeting, or stretch while watching TV. It's about sneaking in movement wherever you can. It's like being a stress-busting ninja, finding opportunities to strike a blow against stress in your everyday life.

The Ripple Effect: More Than Just Stress Relief

Here's the kicker: the benefits ripple out beyond just beating stress. You'll likely sleep better, feel more energized, and boost your overall mood. It's like hitting a jackpot of feel-good vibes. Plus, you'll be rocking that 'I just worked out' glow, and who doesn't love that?

So, let's get moving and grooving! Make physical activity your fun, energetic ally in the fight against stress. It's time to sweat the stress away and dance (or walk, or jog, or yoga) our way to a happier, healthier you. Let's turn stress into sweat and smiles!

Sleep: Your Secret Weapon in the War on Stress

Welcome to the dreamy realm of sleep, the unsung hero in your stress-busting arsenal. Think of a good night's sleep as your body's secret agent, working undercover to fight off stress while you're off in dreamland. It's not just about catching Z's; it's about giving stress the knockout punch.

Sleep: The Ultimate Recharger

Imagine your body and mind as a smartphone. Just like how your phone needs to be plugged in to recharge, your body and mind need sleep to power up. A solid night's sleep is like plugging into a supercharger - you wake up refreshed, rebooted, and ready to take on the world. It's like giving stress a one-two punch and saying, "Not today, stress, not today."

The Magic of ZZZs: More Than Just Rest

When you're snoozing, your body is like a busy little elf, repairing and rejuvenating. It's working hard to balance hormones, repair muscles, and sort through the day's memories. Good sleep can sharpen your brain, boost your mood, and even make you a nicer person to be around (because let's face it, who's chipper on four hours of sleep?).

The Sleep-Stress Dance: A Delicate Balance

Here's the spicy twist: stress and sleep are like dance partners in a tango. Too much stress can make it hard to sleep, and not enough sleep can make you more prone to stress. It's a delicate dance, but once you get the rhythm, it's a beautiful thing.

Creating a Sleep Sanctuary: Your Nightly Retreat

Let's turn your bedroom into a sleep sanctuary. No more scrolling through social media in bed - let's keep screens out of the boudoir. Make your bedroom a cozy retreat - think comfy pillows, a cool, dark environment, and maybe a hint of lavender. It's about creating a nightly ritual that whispers to your body, "Hey, it's time to wind down."

So, let's embrace the power of sleep in our quest to conquer stress. It's time to make sleep a non-negotiable, a sacred ritual, a nightly journey to a stress-free tomorrow. Sweet dreams, stress warriors, and here's to waking up feeling like superheroes ready to save the day!

Chapter 5
Cognitive Approaches to Stress Reduction

Welcome to Chapter 5, where we dive into the mind-bending world of cognitive approaches to stress reduction. Think of this chapter as your mental workout zone, where we flex our brain muscles to lift the heavy weights of stress.

It's time to put on your mental sweatbands and get ready to reshape the way you think about stress.

CBT: Your Brain's Personal Trainer

First up, let's talk about Cognitive Behavioral Therapy (CBT) - it's like having a personal trainer for your thoughts. CBT shows you how to spot those sneaky, stress-inducing thoughts and how to bench-press them into something more positive and empowering. It's about changing the mental tapes that play in your head, turning "I can't handle this!" into "I've got this!"

Reframing: The Art of Mental Makeovers

Next, we'll master the art of reframing negative thoughts. Imagine each negative thought as a gloomy, old painting. Reframing is like adding bright, new colors to that painting, transforming it into something more hopeful and uplifting. It's about seeing the glass as half full, even when life keeps pouring out a little.

MBSR: Your Mindfulness-Based Stress Reduction Toolkit

Then, we'll explore Mindfulness-Based Stress Reduction (MBSR) techniques. This is where we bring mindfulness into the mix, teaching you how to stay grounded and calm, even when stress tries to sweep you off your feet. It's like having an anchor that keeps you steady in the stormy seas of life.

Thought-Challenging Exercises: The Mental Obstacle Course

And for the grand finale, we'll dive into thought-challenging exercises. These are like mental obstacle courses that help you navigate and overcome your stress-inducing thoughts. You'll learn how to question and challenge these thoughts, turning them from scary monsters under the bed into harmless dust bunnies.

By the end of this chapter, you'll be a mental gymnast, flipping and tumbling your stress thoughts into something more manageable and less daunting. So, let's get those mental gears turning and start our journey to a more stress-resilient mindset.

Ready, set, think!

CBT: The Stress-Busting Brain Bootcamp

Welcome to the world of Cognitive Behavioral Therapy (CBT), your new secret weapon in the battle against stress. Think of CBT as a brain bootcamp, where you train your thoughts to be lean, mean, stress-fighting machines. It's not about changing what happens to you; it's about changing how you react to what happens. Let's break it down:

CBT: The Basics

Imagine your brain as a garden. CBT helps you weed out the negative thoughts (those pesky stress weeds) and plant more positive, resilient ones. It's like being a gardener of your mind, cultivating a more peaceful, stress-resistant headspace.

The Stress Thought Trap

Stress often comes from the way we think about things. It's like wearing gloomy glasses that turn even sunny days gray. CBT teaches you to take off those glasses and see the world in a more balanced, less stressful way. It's about spotting those doom-and-gloom thoughts and giving them a reality check.

The CBT Toolbox: Your Mental Toolkit

CBT comes with a toolbox full of techniques. There's the 'thought diary' where you jot down stressy thoughts and challenge them. There's the 'behavioral experiment' where you test out new ways of reacting to stress. And there's the 'problem-solving' technique, where you break down stressors into bite-sized, manageable pieces.

CBT in Action: Real-Life Stress Busting

Let's say traffic jams make you want to tear your hair out. CBT helps you change that script. Instead of thinking, "This is unbearable, I can't stand it!", you learn to tell yourself, "It's just traffic. I can handle this. It's a great time to listen to my favorite podcast."

By the end of this CBT crash course, you'll be equipped with the skills to tackle stress head-on. You'll be like a mental ninja, slicing through stressful thoughts with the precision of a samurai. So, let's get ready to rewire our brains and kick stress to the curb, CBT style!

COGNITIVE APPROACHES TO STRESS REDUCTION

Reframing: Giving Your Negative Thoughts a Makeover

Step right up to the magical world of reframing, where negative thoughts get a dazzling makeover. It's like taking those gloomy, stress-inducing thoughts and flipping them into something brighter and more upbeat.

Reframing isn't about pretending everything is sunshine and rainbows; it's about choosing a more positive, stress-busting perspective. Let's turn those mental frowns upside down!

Spotting the Gloomies

First things first, let's catch those negative Nellies. These are the thoughts that rain on your parade, like "I'll never get this right" or "Everything always goes wrong for me." They're like little clouds of gloom hovering over your head. The trick is to spot them before they turn into a downpour.

The Reframing Magic

Now for the fun part - the reframing! It's like being a word wizard, casting spells to transform thoughts. "I'll never get this right" becomes "I haven't mastered this yet, but I'm getting better every day." "Everything always goes wrong for me" turns into "Sometimes things don't go as planned, and that's okay. I can handle it." It's about finding the silver lining, even in the cloudiest situations.

The Power of Positivity

Reframing is like flexing your positivity muscles. The more you do it, the stronger they get. It's about training your brain to see challenges as opportunities, and setbacks as learning experiences. It's like putting on a pair of rose-tinted glasses that help you see the brighter side of life.

The Ripple Effect

The coolest thing about reframing? It has a ripple effect. When you start flipping your negative thoughts, you'll notice a shift in your mood, your stress levels, even how you interact with others. It's like a positivity pebble thrown into the pond of your life, creating waves of good vibes.

By mastering the art of reframing, you're not just managing stress; you're transforming it.

You're turning those mental stumbling blocks into stepping stones. So, let's start giving those negative thoughts a fabulous new look, one positive twist at a time!

COGNITIVE APPROACHES TO STRESS REDUCTION

Mindfulness-Based Stress Reduction: Your Chill Pill in a Busy World

Welcome to the zen zone of Mindfulness-Based Stress Reduction (MBSR) techniques, where we turn the volume down on life's chaos and tune into the calm channel. MBSR is like having a secret garden in your mind, a peaceful retreat you can visit anytime things get too loud. Let's explore how to tap into this tranquil oasis.

The Here and Now: Mindfulness Magic

Mindfulness is all about living in the here and now, soaking up the present moment like a sponge. It's about noticing the little things - the warmth of the sun on your skin, the taste of your morning coffee, the sound of laughter. It's like pressing pause on life's fast-forward button, savoring the now, not fretting over the past or future.

Breathing: Your Anchor in the Storm

A big part of MBSR is focusing on your breath. It's like finding a calm anchor in the choppy seas of your day. Try this: take a slow, deep breath in, hold it for a moment, and then let it out gently. Feel your chest rise and fall, listen to the sound of your breath - it's like a wave washing over you, clearing away stress.

Body Scan: The Head-to-Toe Chill

The body scan is another cool MBSR trick. Lie down or sit comfortably and slowly focus on each part of your body, from your toes to your head. It's like doing a mental check-in with yourself, releasing tension as you go. Imagine stress melting away from each body part, leaving you relaxed and rejuvenated.

Mindful Moments: Little Pauses of Peace

You can sprinkle mindful moments throughout your day. Take a minute to really savor your lunch, feel the texture, and taste the flavors. Or pause and listen to the sounds around you - birds chirping, leaves rustling. These mini mindfulness breaks are like tiny vacations for your mind.

By weaving MBSR techniques into your daily routine, you're building a fortress of calm in your mind. It's about finding pockets of peace in the hustle and bustle of everyday life.

So, let's embrace mindfulness and turn our days into a series of serene moments, one mindful breath at a time!

Chapter 6
Lifestyle Changes for Stress Management

Welcome to Chapter 6, where we roll up our sleeves and give your lifestyle a fabulous stress-busting makeover! Think of this chapter as your guide to tweaking, twisting, and totally transforming your daily habits into a stress-resistant super routine. We're not just dabbling on the surface; we're diving deep into the nitty-gritty of your everyday life to weed out the stressors and plant seeds of calm and joy.

Eating Your Way to Calm: The Stress-Smashing Diet

First on the menu, we're spicing up your diet with stress-reducing superfoods. It's like turning your meals into mini-meditation sessions. We'll explore foods that are like chill pills for your body, and how a balanced diet can be your secret weapon in the war against stress. Get ready to munch your way to mellow!

Social Buffet: Feasting on Friendships

Next, let's talk about the power of people. Your social connections are like a cozy blanket on a chilly night. We'll dive into how strong support networks can buffer you from stress and how to nurture these relationships. It's about creating a buffet of friendships that nourish your soul.

The Art of Time Juggling: Mastering Your Schedule

Then, we're going to become time management ninjas. It's all about organizing your day so that stress doesn't stand a chance. We'll share strategies to help you juggle your tasks like a circus pro, making sure you're not just busy, but productive. Say goodbye to the chaos and hello to the calm!

The Great Balancing Act: Work and Play

And finally, we'll tackle the ultimate challenge: balancing work and personal life. It's like being a tightrope walker, finding that perfect harmony between 'doing' and 'being'. We'll explore ways to set boundaries, prioritize self-care, and make sure you're living, not just existing.

By the end of this chapter, you'll have a lifestyle that's not just stress-resistant, but stress-busting. You'll be equipped with the tools, tips, and tricks to turn every day into a stress-smashing success.

So, let's get ready to revamp, rejuvenate, and re-energize your life!

Eating Your Way to Zen: The Stress-Busting Diet

Get ready to turn your kitchen into a stress-busting haven! We're about to embark on a culinary adventure where every bite not only tantalizes your taste buds but also sends stress packing. It's time to eat your way to a more chilled-out you!

Superfoods to the Rescue

Let's start with the superheroes of the food world: superfoods. These are the foods that pack a punch in the fight against stress.

Think of them as your edible allies. Foods rich in magnesium, like leafy greens and nuts, are like a chill pill for your body. Omega-3 fatty acids, found in fish like salmon, are like a soothing balm for your brain. And don't forget those colorful fruits and veggies - they're loaded with antioxidants that fight stress like little warriors.

Snack Smart

Snack attacks can be a hidden source of stress. Instead of reaching for that bag of chips, grab a handful of almonds or a piece of dark chocolate. Yes, chocolate! Dark chocolate, in moderation, can help reduce stress. It's like a delicious, guilt-free hug for your brain.

Hydration Nation

Water, water, everywhere, and every drop to drink! Staying hydrated is like giving your body a mini spa treatment. Dehydration can make stress worse, so keep that water bottle handy. Infuse it with some lemon, cucumber, or berries for an extra zing. It's like a spa day in a bottle.

Mindful Eating

Now, let's talk about how you eat. Mindful eating is like a meditation session at the dining table. It's about slowing down, savoring each bite, and really connecting with your food.

Turn off the TV, put down your phone, and give your meal the attention it deserves.

It's not just about what you eat, but how you eat.

Meal Prep Magic

Last but not least, let's get into meal prep. Planning your meals can cut down on stress big time. It's like having a roadmap for your week's eating journey. Spend some time on the weekend chopping, cooking, and storing, and you'll thank yourself during the week. It's like a time machine for your future self.

By incorporating these diet and nutrition tips into your life, you're not just feeding your body; you're nourishing your soul and keeping stress at bay. So, let's turn our meals into a stress-relief fiesta, one delicious bite at a time!

Social Superpowers: Harnessing the Might of Your Tribe

Get ready to dive into the power of people - your secret stress-busting weapon! Social connections and support networks are like your personal cheerleading squad, ready to lift you up when stress tries to pull you down. It's time to tap into the magic of your tribe and turn socializing into your stress shield.

The Strength of the Pack

Think of your social circle as a pack of superheroes, each with their own unique power to help you battle stress. Friends, family, colleagues - they're all part of your stress-fighting team. It's like having a group of sidekicks ready to swoop in when the going gets tough. A heart-to-heart with a friend can be as soothing as a warm blanket on a cold night. A belly laugh with your family can blow away stress like a gust of wind.

Building Your Support Network

Building a strong support network doesn't mean you need a Rolodex full of contacts.

It's about nurturing meaningful connections. It's like planting a garden - it takes time, care, and a bit of love.

Reach out, make plans, be there for others, and let them be there for you. It's a two-way street paved with care and support.

The Digital Connection

In our digital world, don't forget the power of online communities. Join groups or forums that share your interests. It's like having a virtual coffee shop where everyone knows your name.

Just remember, online or offline, quality trumps quantity. It's about deep, meaningful connections, not just the number of friends on your list.

The Healing Power of Helping

Ever heard of the helper's high? Lending a hand to others can actually reduce your stress. It's like a boomerang of goodness - you throw out help, and back comes a wave of feel-good vibes. Volunteer, support a cause, be there for a friend - it's like stress-busting karma in action.

The Art of Saying 'No'

- And here's a spicy little tip: learn the art of saying 'no.' You can't be everything to everyone, and that's okay. Setting boundaries is crucial in maintaining healthy relationships. It's like putting on your oxygen mask first before helping others.

By harnessing the power of social connections and support networks, you're not just managing stress; you're building a fortress against it. So, let's cherish our relationships, nurture our connections, and make our social life a stress-busting powerhouse!

Time Taming: Becoming a Maestro of Your Minutes

Strap in, time tamers! We're about to dive into the art of time management and organization - your secret weapons in the war against stress. It's time to take the reins of your schedule and steer it like a pro. Say goodbye to the chaos and hello to the calm, one well-planned moment at a time.

The Magic of Lists: Your Stress-Busting Scrolls

Let's start with the humble to-do list, a simple yet mighty tool in your time-taming arsenal. It's like having a map for your day. Jot down tasks, big and small, and relish the satisfaction of crossing them off. It's like a mini victory dance for every task you conquer. And hey, if something doesn't get done today, no sweat - there's always tomorrow.

Prioritize Like a Boss

Not all tasks are created equal. It's time to play favorites. Ask yourself, "What's the most important thing I need to tackle today?" Focus on that. It's like being a chef in a busy kitchen - you've got to know which dish to cook first. This way, you're not just busy; you're productive.

The Power of 'No'

Remember, saying 'no' is a superpower. You can't juggle a million things and expect not to drop a few. Be realistic about what you can handle. It's like setting the right weight for your workout - too much, and you'll strain yourself; too little, and you won't feel the benefit.

Declutter Your Space, Declutter Your Mind

A cluttered space is like a cluttered mind.
Take some time to tidy up your workspace, your home, your digital files. It's like doing a detox for your environment. A clean, organized space can work wonders for your mental clarity and stress levels.

Time Buffers: Your Secret Stress Cushion

Here's a spicy tip: build in time buffers. Give yourself extra time between tasks and appointments. It's like having a secret stress cushion, so you're not always rushing from one thing to the next. It's the difference between a leisurely stroll and a frantic sprint.

By mastering these time management and organizational strategies, you're setting yourself up for a smoother, more serene life. You're becoming the maestro of your minutes, orchestrating your days with precision and grace. So, let's get those planners out and start taming time like the stress-busting wizards we are!

The Great Balancing Act: Juggling Work and Play Like a Pro

Welcome to the high-wire act of balancing work and personal life, where we learn to juggle responsibilities without dropping the ball. It's time to become a master juggler, keeping your work, family, and personal time in harmonious motion. Say goodbye to the tug-of-war and hello to a life of balance and bliss!

Setting Boundaries: Your Invisible Superpower

First up, let's talk boundaries. They're like invisible force fields that protect your personal time from being invaded by work. Set clear limits on when you work and when you unplug. It's like putting up a "Do Not Disturb" sign on your personal life. When the workday ends, let it really end. No sneaky emails during dinner or thinking about reports at your kid's soccer game.

Quality Time vs. Quantity Time

Remember, it's not about how much time you spend, but how you spend it. Make your personal time count. Be fully present with your loved ones, like you're the star of your own movie. Whether it's a 15-minute coffee break with a friend or a weekend getaway, make those moments shine.

The Art of Delegation: Not a One-Person Show

You don't have to be the superhero in every scene. Delegate tasks at work and share responsibilities at home. It's like being a director who trusts their cast.

Delegating allows you to focus on what you do best and gives others a chance to shine too.

Self-Care: Your Personal Pit Stop

Don't forget the pit stops - self-care is crucial. It's like pulling your car over for a tune-up. Take time for activities that recharge your batteries. Yoga, reading, a bubble bath, or just a quiet walk - find what refuels you and make it a non-negotiable part of your routine.

Flexibility: The Secret Ingredient

And finally, be flexible. Balancing work and personal life isn't a rigid tightrope walk; it's more like a dance. Sometimes you lean more one way, sometimes the other. It's about finding a rhythm that works for you, and being okay with adjusting it as you go.

By mastering the art of balancing work and personal life, you're setting the stage for a happier, healthier you. It's about giving each aspect of your life its time to shine, without letting one overshadow the other. So, let's embrace this balancing act with open arms and dance our way to a beautifully balanced life!

Chapter 7
Alternative and Complementary Stress Relief Methods

Welcome to Chapter 7, where we dive into the colorful and exciting world of alternative and complementary stress relief methods. Think of this chapter as your all-access pass to a buffet of unconventional chill-out techniques. It's time to mix, match, and sample a variety of fun and unique ways to send stress packing and invite relaxation in. Let's explore these cool, quirky, and oh-so-soothing practices!

Yoga and Tai Chi: Your Body's Peaceful Warriors

First up, let's stretch into the world of Yoga and Tai Chi. These aren't just exercises; they're like moving meditations. Imagine bending, stretching, and flowing your way to tranquility.

Yoga and Tai Chi are like giving your body a gentle hug while telling your mind to take a chill pill.

They're all about balance, harmony, and finding a zen state in every pose or movement.

Aromatherapy: The Sweet Smell of Serenity

Next, let's take a whiff of the aromatic world of essential oils and aromatherapy. It's like having a spa in your pocket. Lavender for relaxation, peppermint to perk up, or eucalyptus to clear the mind - each scent is a key to unlocking different moods and sensations. It's about turning your home or workspace into a stress-free sanctuary, one sniff at a time.

Music and Art Therapy: Unleashing Your Inner Artist

And then, there's the magical realm of music and art therapy. These aren't just hobbies; they're your secret escape routes from stress. Imagine painting your worries away or singing stress into submission.

Music and art therapy are about expressing what's inside, even when words fail you. It's like channeling your inner Picasso or Beethoven to combat stress.

In this chapter, we're going to explore, experiment, and embrace these alternative methods. They're like adding a dash of spice to your stress management recipe - a little unconventional, a lot effective, and a whole lot of fun. So, let's get ready to stretch, sniff, and create our way to a calmer, more centered you!

Yoga and Tai Chi: The Dynamic Duo of Serenity

Welcome to the serene world of Yoga and Tai Chi, where every move is a step towards tranquility. These aren't just physical exercises; they're like a dance with peace and calm. Let's dive into how these ancient practices can be your modern-day superheroes in the fight against stress.

Yoga: Your Flexible Friend in Stress Relief

Picture Yoga as a blend of stretching, strength, and deep breathing - all rolled into one. It's like giving your body a gentle wake-up call, stretching out the kinks and knots of stress. From the mountain pose to the downward dog, each posture is a step towards inner peace. Yoga is like a battery charger for your body and soul. It boosts your flexibility, strengthens your muscles, and calms your mind. It's like hitting the refresh button on your entire being.

Tai Chi: The Slow-Motion Magic

Now, let's glide into the world of Tai Chi. Imagine performing martial arts in slow motion, like a graceful dance with the air. Tai Chi is all about slow, deliberate movements combined with deep breathing. It's like meditating while moving. Each gesture is a flow of energy, a gentle wave that washes away stress and leaves a sea of calm in its wake. Tai Chi is a powerhouse for reducing stress, improving balance, and enhancing mental focus. It's like whispering to your body, "Hey, let's take it easy."

The Shared Benefits: Body and Mind Harmony

Both Yoga and Tai Chi are champions in harmonizing body and mind. They teach you to breathe through the stress, to move with intention, and to find stillness in motion. It's about being present in the moment, fully engaged with every breath and movement. These practices are like a duo of detectives, uncovering the hidden stress in your body and gently coaxing it out.

By incorporating Yoga and Tai Chi into your life, you're signing up for a journey of self-discovery and stress relief. They're like your personal trainers, guiding you towards a more peaceful, centered version of yourself. So, let's roll out the mat, step into the flow, and embrace the gentle power of Yoga and Tai Chi!

ALTERNATIVE AND COMPLEMENTARY STRESS RELIEF METHODS

Aromatherapy: The Scent-sational Way to De-Stress

Welcome to the fragrant world of aromatherapy, where each sniff is a step towards serenity. Imagine turning your home into a stress-free sanctuary, just with the power of scents.

Essential oils aren't just pretty smells; they're like your personal relaxation assistants, ready to soothe, uplift, and unwind your mind.

The Essence of Relaxation: Essential Oils 101

Essential oils are like the superheroes of the plant world, each with their own special powers. Lavender is the queen of calm, a whiff can send stress packing and invite in peace. Peppermint is a zesty energy booster, perfect for when you need a pick-me-up. Eucalyptus? It's like a breath of fresh air for your mind, clearing the mental fog.

Your DIY Spa Experience

Transform your home into a DIY spa with just a few drops of these magical oils. Add them to a diffuser and let the aroma fill your space. It's like having an invisible stress shield around you. You can also add a few drops to your bath, letting the warm water and soothing scents wash away the worries of the day. It's like soaking in a pool of tranquility.

On-the-Go Peace: Portable Relaxation

And the best part? You can take this aromatic bliss with you. A drop of oil on your wrist or a scented handkerchief can be your secret stress-busting weapon in a busy day. It's like carrying a little bottle of peace in your pocket.

The Scented Sleep Hack

Let's not forget the bedtime benefits. A dab of lavender on your pillow or a chamomile-scented room spray can set the stage for a night of sweet, stress-free dreams. It's like sending an invitation to the Sandman for a peaceful night's sleep.

By embracing the world of aromatherapy and essential oils, you're adding a splash of scent-sational magic to your stress management toolkit. It's a simple, delightful, and effective way to ease tension and enhance your well-being. So, let's get ready to sniff our way to a more relaxed and joyful you!

ALTERNATIVE AND COMPLEMENTARY STRESS RELIEF METHODS

Music and Art Therapy: Jamming and Painting Away the Stress

Step into the vibrant world of music and art therapy, where creativity is your ally in the battle against stress. Imagine channeling your inner stress into a masterpiece or a melody. These aren't just hobbies; they're your secret weapons for serenity.

Let's crank up the tunes and splash some color to keep stress at bay!

Music Therapy: Your Personal Stress Soundtrack

Dive into the rhythm of music therapy, where every beat and note is a step away from stress. It's like having a personal soundtrack for your mood. Feeling tense? Try some soothing classical music or gentle jazz to smooth out those stress wrinkles.

Need an energy boost?

Pump up some upbeat tunes and dance the stress away. Music therapy is like a DJ mixing the perfect tracks to tune your emotions.

Art Therapy: Painting Your Worries Away

Now, let's grab some brushes and colors for a session of art therapy. It's not about creating a masterpiece for a gallery; it's about expressing what's inside you. Splash your feelings onto a canvas, doodle your worries away, or sculpt your stress into clay. Art therapy is like having a visual conversation with yourself, where colors and shapes do the talking. It's a way to let your inner world out, to see and understand your stress in a new light.

The Healing Power of Creativity

Engaging in music and art therapy is like giving your mind a playground to run free. It's a break from the usual stress scripts, a chance to get lost in the flow of creating. This creative flow is a powerful stress reliever - it's like stepping into a different world where stress doesn't exist, even if just for a moment.

No Experience Required

And the best part? You don't need to be Mozart or Picasso. It's all about the process, not the product. Strum a guitar, hit some keys on a piano, or just hum along to a tune. Grab some crayons, make a collage, or just splash paint around. It's about letting your creativity flow, not about judging the outcome.

By incorporating music and art therapy into your life, you're unlocking new, joyful ways to manage stress. It's about turning your emotions into art, your worries into melodies.

So, let's get ready to create, play, and sing our way to a stress-free zone!

Chapter 8

Interviews with Experts

Welcome to Chapter 8, where we roll out the red carpet for the maestros of stress management! This chapter is like a backstage pass to the world of stress-busting wisdom. We've lined up interviews with psychologists, health pros, and real-life stress conquerors who've turned their battles into victories. It's a treasure trove of insights, tips, and real-world wisdom that's as spicy as it is enlightening.

Chatting with Psychologists: Unpacking the Stress Suitcase

- First up, we're sitting down with psychologists to unpack the hefty suitcase of stress. These are the folks who study stress like detectives, understanding its sneaky ways. They'll share secrets on how stress works in the brain and offer up strategies to outsmart it. It's like getting a masterclass in stress psychology, minus the homework.

Health Pros Spill the Beans: Stress-Busting Health Hacks

Next, we're tapping into the brains of health professionals. They're the front-line warriors in the battle against stress, armed with tips and tricks to keep your body and mind in top shape. From diet do's and don'ts to exercise eurekas, they're dishing out advice that's as practical as it is powerful.

Real-Life Stress Victories: Tales from the Trenches

And then, the real gems: stories from people just like you and me who've wrestled with stress and come out on top. These aren't fairy tales; they're real-life chronicles of triumph over tension. Hear how they turned stress from a monster under the bed into a mouse in the corner. It's like having a chat with a friend who's been there, done that, and got the stress-free T-shirt.

So, buckle up for a chapter filled with enlightenment, empowerment, and expert advice. We're diving deep into the world of stress management, guided by those who know it best.

Get ready for some eye-opening conversations and a whole lot of "Aha!" moments!

MIND MASTERS: PSYCHOLOGISTS SPILL THE SECRETS ON STRESS

Get ready to dive into the minds of psychologists, the Sherlock Holmeses of the stress world. We've had some spicy chats with these brain buffs, and they're here to spill the beans on all things stress. It's like getting a backstage pass to the inner workings of your mind under pressure.

The Stress Blueprint: Understanding the Enemy

First off, these mind maestros walk us through what stress really is. It's like they've drawn a blueprint of this invisible troublemaker. They explain how stress is like your body's alarm system - sometimes useful, but you don't want it going off all the time. It's about understanding this alarm, so you're not jumping every time it rings.

The Brain Under Siege: What's Really Going On Up There

Next, they take us on a tour of the brain on stress. Imagine your brain as a busy office, and stress is like an unexpected fire drill - everything goes haywire for a bit. They break down how stress affects your thoughts, feelings, and even your decision-making skills. It's like getting a user manual for your brain under stress.

The Great Stress Myths: Busting the Legends

Then, we get into some myth-busting. Psychologists debunk common stress misconceptions. No, stress isn't always bad. Yes, you can harness it for good. It's like they're shining a light on stress's biggest secrets, turning scary shadows into manageable challenges.

Tools and Tricks: The Psychologist's Stress Toolbox

And here's the gold: psychologists share their top tools and tricks for managing stress.

They talk about techniques like mindfulness, cognitive reframing, and even simple breathing exercises. It's like getting a stress-busting toolkit, customized by the experts.

By the end of these conversations, you'll feel like you've had a coffee chat with the brainy best. Psychologists offer insights that are not just smart but also super practical. So, let's soak up this wisdom and turn their words into our stress-busting weapons!

Health Gurus Unleash: Stress-Busting Wisdom for the Win

Strap in for a whirlwind tour of insights from the crème de la crème of health professionals. These wellness wizards have opened their treasure chests of knowledge, and they're ready to share their top tips for kicking stress to the curb. It's like getting a VIP pass to the best health hacks in town!

The Body-Stress Connection: Tuning into Your Temple

First up, these health pros dive into how stress is a bit of a party crasher in your body. It's like an uninvited guest that can mess with everything from your heart to your gut. They share how tuning into your body's signals is like having an early warning system for stress. It's about catching stress before it turns your body into a stress-themed amusement park.

Eat, Sleep, Breathe: The Health Trifecta

Then, they dish out advice on the big three: eating, sleeping, and breathing. It's like learning the ABCs of stress management. They talk about foods that are like natural stress relievers, how sleep is your body's secret weapon against stress, and why breathing is not just something you do to stay alive, but a powerful tool to stay calm.

Move It to Lose It: Stress-Busting Through Exercise

Get ready to sweat the stress away! These health gurus are big fans of using exercise as a stress buster. It's not just about getting fit; it's about moving your way to a more relaxed state. Whether it's yoga, running, or just a brisk walk, they share how physical activity is like hitting the reset button on your stress levels.

Mind Over Matter: The Power of Positive Thinking

And here's the mental magic - they delve into the power of positive thinking and mental resilience. It's like putting on a pair of glasses that helps you see the world in a more stress-free way.

They share strategies for changing your thought patterns, so you're not just reacting to stress, but actively managing it.

By the end of these enlightening chats, you'll feel like you've been to a wellness workshop with the best in the biz. These health professionals don't just understand stress; they know how to beat it at its own game. So, let's take these gems of wisdom and polish them into our own stress-busting strategies!

STRESS TRIUMPHS: REAL PEOPLE, REAL VICTORIES

Buckle up for a rollercoaster ride of real-life stress triumphs! We've gathered stories from everyday heroes who've wrestled with stress and pinned it to the mat. These aren't fairy tales; they're raw, real, and relatable sagas of people turning stress from a monster into a mouse.

It's like having a heart-to-heart with friends who've been in the stress trenches and climbed out, victorious.

The Comeback Kid: Turning Stress into Success

Meet the Comeback Kid, who turned a job loss into an opportunity for a dream career. It's a tale of resilience, of using stress as a springboard to leap into the unknown and land on their feet. They share how embracing change, rather than fearing it, turned stress into a launchpad for success.

The Zen Master Mom: Juggling Kids and Calm

Then there's the story of the Zen Master Mom, who managed to find peace amidst the chaos of parenting. She's like a ninja of calm in a world of toys, tantrums, and timeouts. Her secret weapons? Mindfulness, a wicked sense of humor, and the art of letting go. It's a masterclass in turning the mayhem of motherhood into moments of zen.

The Office Yogi: Breathing Through Deadlines

Enter the Office Yogi, whose tale of tackling workplace stress is nothing short of inspiring. Stuck in a cycle of endless meetings and tight deadlines, they found solace in deep breathing and lunchtime yoga. It's a story of transforming a cubicle into a haven of tranquility, one deep breath at a time.

The Silver Linings Story: Finding Joy in the Small Things

And let's not forget the Silver Linings Story, where a battle with illness led to a newfound appreciation for life's little joys. This story is a poignant reminder of how stress can shift our perspective, teaching us to find happiness in the here and now, to cherish the small things that we often overlook.

These stories are like beacons of hope, shining a light on the path through the fog of stress. They remind us that stress, no matter how daunting, can be tamed, managed, and even transformed. So, let's soak in these tales of triumph and use them as fuel to write our own success stories in the book of stress management!

Chapter 9
Developing Your Personal Stress Management Plan

Welcome to the grand finale, Chapter 9, where we roll up our sleeves and get down to business crafting your very own Stress Management Plan.

Think of this as your personal recipe for chill, a custom-made guide tailored to fit your unique lifestyle, quirks, and all. It's time to transform what you've learned into a daily routine that keeps stress at bay and brings in a wave of calm.

Building Your Stress-Busting Toolkit

We're starting with the essentials - building a toolkit that's as unique as you are. It's like picking out the coolest gadgets for your stress-busting utility belt. From deep breathing exercises to power walks, from mindful moments to gratitude journals, we'll guide you in choosing the tools that resonate with you. It's about creating a mix that's just right - not too spicy, not too mild, but perfect for your taste.

Consistency is Key: Keeping the Momentum Going

Next, we'll dive into the art of consistency. Let's face it, even the best plans can fizzle out without a little stick-to-itiveness. We'll share tips on how to make your stress management routine as natural as brushing your teeth. It's about finding your rhythm, setting reminders, and maybe even roping in a buddy for that extra nudge. It's like setting up a daily date with calm, and you're not standing it up!

Customizing Your Plan: One Size Does Not Fit All

And here's where it gets really fun - personalizing your plan. Your life, your rules. Night owl or early bird, couch potato or gym rat, we've got you covered. We'll help you tailor your stress management routine to fit into your life, not the other way around. It's like being a chef in your own stress-relief kitchen, tweaking the recipe until it's just right.

By the end of this chapter, you'll have a stress management plan that's as unique as your fingerprint. It's your secret weapon, your personal chill pill, ready to be deployed whenever stress rears its ugly head. So, let's get ready to craft, customize, and conquer stress, one personalized plan at a time!

DEVELOPING YOUR PERSONAL STRESS
MANAGEMENT PLAN

Cooking Up Your Stress-Relief Recipe: Crafting the Perfect Routine

Alright, let's whip up your stress management routine, a recipe for relaxation that's as unique and fabulous as you are. Think of it as cooking your favorite dish - a pinch of this, a dash of that, all tailored to your taste. Here's how to create a routine that zaps stress and brings in buckets of bliss.

Step 1: Know Your Ingredients (Identify Your Stressors)

First things first, let's identify your stressors. It's like picking out the ingredients for your stress-relief stew. What really gets your pot boiling? Work deadlines? Family chaos? Traffic jams?

Knowing what cranks up your stress is the first step in figuring out how to dial it back down.

Step 2: Choose Your Tools (Select Your Techniques)

Now, let's select your tools - the techniques that'll help you simmer down. Maybe it's yoga for some, a brisk walk for others, or perhaps a few minutes of deep breathing. It's about finding what works for you. Like choosing between a spatula or a whisk, pick the tools that fit your cooking style.

Step 3: Timing is Everything (Set a Routine)

Timing is crucial. Just like you wouldn't bake a cake at 500 degrees for 10 minutes, you need to time your stress management routine right. Slot in quick stress-busting activities throughout your day - a morning meditation, a lunchtime walk, an evening journaling session. It's about spreading out the stress relief to keep the heat at a steady, manageable level.

Step 4: Spice It Up (Keep It Interesting

Variety is the spice of life, and it's also the spice of a good stress management routine. Mix it up! Maybe try mindfulness one day and aromatherapy the next. Keeping your routine interesting prevents it from becoming just another chore. It's like adding a new seasoning to your favorite dish to give it an exciting twist.

Step 5: Taste Test (Evaluate and Adjust)

Finally, don't forget to taste test. After trying out your routine for a while, ask yourself, "Is this working? Do I feel less stressed?" If something's not to your liking, tweak it. Swap it out. Add something new.

Your stress management routine should be a living, breathing thing that evolves with you.

By following these guidelines, you'll cook up a stress management routine that's as satisfying as your favorite comfort food. It's about finding the right balance of ingredients, tools, and timing to create a dish - I mean, a plan - that keeps stress on the back burner and turns up the flavor on relaxation and joy. Let's get cooking!

Keeping the Chill Vibes Rolling: Staying Consistent and Motivated

Alright, stress-busters, let's talk about keeping the groove going. Consistency and motivation are the secret sauce to making your stress management routine stick. It's like keeping the beat in a catchy tune - you don't want to lose the rhythm. Here are some hot tips to keep you on track and your stress levels on the down-low.

Tip 1: Make It as Routine as Morning Coffee

Let's weave your stress-busting activities into your daily routine. Make them as non-negotiable as your morning cup of joe. Whether it's a five-minute breathing exercise or a quick stroll around the block, slot it into your daily schedule. It's about making stress management a regular part of your day, not just an afterthought.

Tip 2: Set Reminders: Your Personal Cheerleaders

In the world of smartphones and gadgets, let's use technology to our advantage. Set reminders or alarms - little nudges that say, "Hey, it's time to de-stress!" It's like having a personal cheerleader in your pocket, rooting for your peace of mind.

Tip 3: Variety is the Spice of Life

Keep things spicy! Mix up your routine to keep it fresh and exciting. Alternate between different activities - yoga today, journaling tomorrow, a nature walk the next day. It's like having a playlist for your stress management, and every day is a new track.

Tip 4: Track Your Progress: The Satisfaction of Seeing Results

There's nothing quite like seeing the fruits of your labor. Keep a simple log or journal of your stress management activities and how you feel after doing them. Over time, you'll see patterns and progress, which is a huge motivator. It's like taking a selfie of your stress levels - before and after.

Tip 5: Buddy Up: Share the Journey

Everything's more fun with a buddy, including stress management. Pair up with a friend or family member. Share your goals and keep each other accountable. It's like having a workout buddy, but for your mental fitness.

Tip 6: Celebrate the Wins, No Matter How Small

And lastly, celebrate your victories. Managed to meditate three times this week? Awesome! Took a deep breath instead of losing your cool in traffic? High five! Celebrating the small wins keeps your spirits up and motivation high. It's like giving yourself a pat on the back - because you deserve it.

By sticking to these tips, you'll keep your stress management routine alive and kicking. It's about building habits, enjoying the journey, and celebrating the wins along the way. So, let's keep the momentum going and turn stress management into a part of your daily rhythm!

DEVELOPING YOUR PERSONAL STRESS MANAGEMENT PLAN

Tailoring Your Stress-Busting Suit: Custom Fit for Your Life

Time to get crafty and tailor your stress management techniques to fit your unique lifestyle and needs like a glove. One size does not fit all in the world of stress relief. It's about stitching together a plan that's as unique as your fingerprint. Let's get into how you can personalize your stress-busting strategies to match your life's rhythm and groove.

Tip 1: Know Thyself: Your Personal Stress Profile

Start by getting up close and personal with your stress. Are you a morning grump or an evening worrier? Does a packed calendar freak you out, or is it an empty to-do list that sends you spiraling?

Understanding your stress patterns is like having a map to your treasure trove of calm.

Tip 2: Match Your Interests: Align with Your Joy

Pick stress-busting activities that align with what you love. If you're a nature lover, your stress relief could be a walk in the park. More of a bookworm? Try unwinding with a good read. Love to move? Dance or exercise might be your go-to. It's about syncing your stress management with your passions.

Tip 3: Fit It Into Your Schedule: No Overhauls Needed

Your stress management routine shouldn't feel like a chore or an added burden. Slot it into your existing schedule. Got a busy morning routine? How about a five-minute meditation while your coffee brews? Long commute? Try some deep breathing or audiobooks to turn traffic time into your chill time.

Tip 4: Home or Away: Location, Location, Location

Consider where you are most of the day. Stuck at a desk? Desk yoga or stretching might be your thing. Always on the move? Mindful walking or audio-guided relaxation can be your go-to. It's about making your environment work for you, not against you.

Tip 5: Trial and Error: The Spice of Life

Don't be afraid to experiment. Try different techniques and see what sticks. Maybe journaling sounded great but felt meh in practice. That's okay! Swap it out for something else. It's like trying on different outfits - some you love, some not so much.

Tip 6: Listen to Your Body and Mind

And most importantly, listen to yourself. How do you feel after each activity? More relaxed? Less tense? Use your body and mind's feedback to tweak and fine-tune your routine. It's like being a DJ for your own stress management - keep adjusting until you find that perfect mix.

By personalizing your stress management techniques, you're crafting a routine that's as unique as you are. It's about embracing your individuality and creating a stress relief plan that fits into your life seamlessly. So, let's get creative and stitch together a plan that's just right for you - your very own stress-busting suit, tailor-made for comfort and style!

Conclusion

The Stress-Busting Wrap-Up: Your Journey to Chilltown

And just like that, we're at the finish line of our stress-busting marathon! But hey, this isn't a goodbye; it's more of a 'see you later' as you continue your journey to becoming a master of chill. Let's do a quick victory lap and wrap up all the spicy, punchy wisdom we've gathered.

THE STRESS MANAGEMENT MIXTAPE: KEY TAKEAWAYS

Think of this book as your personal stress management mixtape, packed with hits from start to finish. We've explored everything from deep breathing to yoga, from mindful eating to the power of a good night's sleep. Remember, managing stress is like cooking your favorite dish - it's all about finding the right ingredients that work for you.

KEEP THE GROOVE GOING: PRACTICE MAKES PERFECT

Now, the real magic happens when you keep the groove going.

It's about making these techniques a part of your daily rhythm, like your favorite catchy tune that you just can't stop humming.

YOUR STRESS-BUSTING LIBRARY: FURTHER RESOURCES

- And if you're hungry for more, there's a whole library of resources out there. From mindfulness apps to stress management workshops, from online forums to wellness podcasts - the world is your oyster. Keep exploring, keep learning, and keep growing.

A PAT ON THE BACK: YOU'VE GOT THIS!

Give yourself a pat on the back; you've come a long way. Remember, managing stress isn't about being perfect; it's about making small, consistent changes that add up to big results. You've got the tools, the techniques, and the know-how. Now, it's all about putting them into action.

So, as we close this chapter (literally), remember that your journey to a less stressed, more blissful life is just beginning. Keep flipping back through these pages whenever you need a reminder or a boost. You've got this, stress warrior!

THE GRAND FINALE: YOUR STRESS-BUSTING ENCORE

As we hit the final note of our stress-busting symphony, let's do a quick boogie through the key takeaways and sprinkle some encouragement for your ongoing journey to master the art of chill.

THE STRESS-BUSTING HIGHLIGHTS REEL: KEY TAKEAWAYS

- Remember, stress is like that uninvited guest at your party - you can't always stop it from showing up, but you sure can decide how long it stays. We've armed you with a toolbox of techniques, from deep breathing to Tai Chi, from mindful munching to the power of a good laugh.

Think of these strategies as your personal stress-busting playlist. You've got tracks for all moods and moments - a tune for when you're feeling overwhelmed, a melody for when you need a pick-me-up, and a rhythm to keep you grooving through your day.

The big message? You're the DJ of your stress levels. You've got the power to turn the volume down on stress and crank up the tunes of tranquility and joy.

- Now, let's talk about keeping the momentum. Like any good habit, stress management gets easier and more effective the more you practice. It's like building a muscle - the more you work it, the stronger it gets.

- Don't sweat the small stuff. Some days, you'll nail your stress management routine; other days, not so much. And that's totally okay. It's not about being perfect; it's about making progress, one chill step at a time.

- Celebrate your victories, no matter how small. Managed to take five deep breaths in a stressful moment? That's a win! Chose a salad over fast food for lunch? Another win! These little victories add up to big changes.

As we wrap up this stress-busting journey, remember that every day is a new opportunity to practice, learn, and grow. You've got a whole arsenal of techniques at your fingertips, ready to help you dance through life's stresses. Keep practicing, keep experimenting, and most importantly, keep smiling.

You've got this, and the world of stress management is cheering you on!

YOUR STRESS-BUSTING TOOLKIT: EXTRA GOODIES FOR YOUR JOURNEY

As we put a bow on our stress-busting adventure, let's not forget that the road to chill-town is filled with many more exciting stops and treasures. To keep your journey spicy and full of zest, here's a roundup of additional resources. Think of these as your bonus tracks, extra spices, and secret ingredients to add to your stress management recipe.

BOOKS THAT SPEAK TO YOUR SOUL

Dive into some page-turners that are all about managing stress and finding balance. Titles like ***The Stress Solution*** by Dr. Rangan Chatterjee or ***Wherever You Go, There You Are*** by Jon Kabat-Zinn are like having a wise guru at your bedside. They're packed with insights, stories, and strategies that can light up your path to peace.

PODCASTS: YOUR ON-THE-GO STRESS GURUS

Plug into some podcasts that are like having a personal stress coach in your ears. Check out shows like ***The Calm Collective*** or ***The Anxiety Coaches Podcast***. Whether you're commuting, jogging, or just chilling on your couch, these podcasts can be your companions in de-stressing.

APPS: YOUR DIGITAL STRESS-BUSTING SIDEKICKS

In this digital age, don't overlook the power of apps. Mindfulness apps like ***Headspace*** or ***Calm*** offer guided meditations, sleep stories, and more. They're like having a mini-retreat in your pocket, ready to help you unwind at the tap of a screen.

ONLINE COMMUNITIES: YOUR VIRTUAL CHEER SQUAD

Join online forums or communities focused on stress management and wellness. Platforms like Reddit or specific Facebook groups can be goldmines for support, advice, and shared experiences. It's like being part of a global stress-busting tribe.

WORKSHOPS AND CLASSES: LEARNING IN ACTION

Keep an eye out for workshops or classes in your area (or online). Whether it's a yoga retreat, a mindfulness workshop, or a stress management seminar, these are great opportunities to learn new techniques and meet fellow stress-busters.

Armed with these additional resources, your journey towards mastering stress doesn't just end here; it evolves. Keep exploring, keep learning, and remember, the world is full of tools and treasures to help you on your path to peace. So, go forth, keep your stress levels in check, and turn every day into a stress-busting fiesta!

APPENDICES

The Stress-Busting Treasure Chest: Your Go-To Goodies and Guides

Welcome to the Appendices, the cherry on top of our stress-busting sundae! This is where we've packed in all the extra goodies, the nifty tools, and the practical guides to keep your stress management journey zesty and fun. Think of this section as your personal stress-busting toolkit, brimming with resources, worksheets, and directories to help you navigate the waves of everyday stress. Let's dive into this treasure chest and discover the gems inside!

Your Stress-Busting Arsenal: Resources and Tools

Here, you'll find a curated list of resources and tools that are like your allies in the battle against stress. From calming apps to insightful books, from soothing music playlists to helpful websites, we've got you covered. It's like having a Swiss Army knife for stress - versatile, handy, and always there when you need it.

Worksheets and Activities: Your Interactive Stress Shields

Get ready to roll up your sleeves and dive into worksheets and activities designed to tackle stress head-on. *These are your interactive guides to understanding, managing, and waving goodbye to stress.* They're fun, they're engaging, and they're incredibly effective. It's like having a personal stress workout, strengthening your chill muscles one activity at a time.

Directory of Pros: Your Stress Relief Squad

- And for times when you need a little extra help, we've included a directory of professional help and support groups. Whether it's a therapist, a counselor, or a support group, having the right people in your corner can make all the difference. It's like having a team of stress-relief superheroes on speed dial.

So, as you flip through these appendices, remember that you're not alone on this journey. You've got a whole arsenal of tools, a bunch of fun activities, and a network of professionals and peers at your fingertips. Use these resources to keep your stress management journey fresh, effective, and tailored just for you. Here's to continuing your adventure in stress-busting with confidence and a whole lot of pizzazz!

Your Stress-Busting Arsenal: Packed with Power Tools

Alright, stress warriors, let's dive into the treasure trove of resources and tools that are going to arm you in your quest for peace and calm. This is your go-to kit, packed with everything you need to tackle stress like a pro. It's like having a superhero utility belt for your mental well-being!

Apps to Zap Stress

- In the digital age, your smartphone can be a sanctuary of calm. Apps like *Headspace* and *Calm* are like having a meditation guru in your pocket. They offer guided meditations, soothing soundscapes, and even bedtime stories to lull you into serenity. It's like a stress relief center at your fingertips.

Books That Speak to Your Soul

For the bookworms, we've got a lineup of reads that are like comfort food for your mind. Titles like ***The Stress Solution*** by Dr. Rangan Chatterjee or ***10% Happier*** by Dan Harris offer insights, personal stories, and practical tips to manage stress. It's like having a heart-to-heart with a wise friend who's been there, done that.

Journals and Planners

Never underestimate the power of a good journal or planner.

Writing down your thoughts, plans, and worries can be incredibly therapeutic. It's like having a conversation with yourself, laying out your stressors on paper, and tackling them one by one.

Plus, planners can help you organize your life, keeping the chaos at bay.

Relaxing Music and Soundscapes

Sometimes, all you need is the right soundtrack to set the mood for relaxation.

It's like creating an audio bubble of calm around you, shielding you from the hustle and bustle.

Yoga Mats and Exercise Gear

For those who find peace in movement, a good yoga mat or some basic exercise gear can be your best friend.

Whether it's stretching, yoga, or a quick workout, having the right equipment can motivate you to take that much-needed me-time.

It's like laying out a welcome mat for relaxation and physical well-being.

With these resources and tools in your stress-busting arsenal, you're well-equipped to face whatever stressors come your way. It's about finding what works for you and making it a part of your daily routine.

So, gear up, get set, and let's keep stress at bay with style and a smile! 🌟 📱 📚 🎵 🧘

The Stress-Busting Workbook: Fun Sheets and Cool Activities

Welcome to the fun zone of stress management - a place where worksheets and activities turn the serious business of stress-busting into a playful adventure. Think of these as your interactive tools, like mini-games for your mind and soul, designed to tackle stress with a dash of fun and a splash of creativity. Let's jump into some of these engaging activities that are as enjoyable as they are effective!

THE STRESS DETECTIVE WORKSHEET

Grab your magnifying glass and play detective with your stress. This worksheet is all about tracking your stress levels throughout the day. Note down what triggered your stress, how you felt, and what you did about it. It's like being a stress sleuth, uncovering clues and patterns to better manage your reactions.

The Gratitude Journal Page

Flip the script on stress with a gratitude journal page. Each day, jot down three things you're grateful for. It could be as simple as a sunny day, a delicious cup of coffee, or a good book. This activity is like a daily dose of positive vibes, shifting your focus from stress to joy.

The Relaxation Response Guide

Here's a step-by-step guide to mastering the relaxation response. It walks you through deep breathing, muscle relaxation, and visualization techniques. It's like having a personal relaxation coach guiding you to a state of calm.

THE RELAXATION RESPONSE GUIDE WORKSHEET

Welcome to Your Personal Relaxation Journey!

This guide is your roadmap to mastering the relaxation response. It's a simple yet powerful way to help your body combat stress. Follow these steps to unlock a state of calm and tranquility.

Step 1: Find Your Quiet Space

- Choose a quiet, comfortable place where you won't be disturbed.
- Sit or lie down in a relaxed position.
- Close your eyes and let go of any distractions.

Step 2: Deep Breathing

- Slowly inhale through your nose, counting to five. Feel your chest and belly rise.
- Hold your breath for a count of three.
- Exhale slowly through your mouth for a count of five. Feel the tension leaving your body with each breath out.
- Repeat this breathing pattern for a few minutes.

Step 3: Progressive Muscle Relaxation

- Start at your feet and work your way up to your head.
- Tense each muscle group for five seconds, then relax for 30 seconds. Notice the contrast between tension and relaxation.
- Move to the next muscle group (calves, thighs, hips, stomach, chest, arms, hands, neck, and face).
- Focus on the sensation of release in each muscle.

Step 4: Visualization

- Imagine a peaceful scene. It could be a beach, a forest, a quiet garden, or any place that makes you feel calm.
- Visualize the details of this place - the sights, sounds, and smells.
- Picture yourself in this serene environment, feeling completely relaxed and at peace.
- Spend a few minutes enjoying this mental escape.

Step 5: Returning to the Moment

- Gently bring your awareness back to the present.
- Wiggle your fingers and toes, stretch your muscles.
- Open your eyes when you feel ready.
- Take a moment to appreciate the calm and relaxation you've achieved.

Reflection

- How do you feel after this exercise?
- What worked well for you? What might you change next time?
- Remember, relaxation is a skill that gets better with practice. Keep using this guide to deepen your relaxation response.

CONGRATULATIONS ON COMPLETING YOUR RELAXATION SESSION!

Keep this guide handy and turn to it whenever you need a moment of peace and tranquility. You're on your way to mastering the art of relaxation! 🌿✨🧘

The Mindfulness Coloring Sheets

Unleash your inner artist with mindfulness coloring sheets. Coloring isn't just for kids; it's a fantastic way to focus your mind and relax. Choose from intricate patterns or simple designs, and let the colors flow. It's like a mini-meditative escape in the middle of your day.

1. Nature's Calm

Purpose: To immerse yourself in the tranquility of nature while coloring.

2. Mandala Magic

Purpose: Mandalas are known for their meditative qualities. Focusing on repetitive patterns can be a great way to practice mindfulness.

3. Ocean Odyssey

Purpose: The fluidity of water and marine life can be soothing to color, offering a sense of peace and connection to nature.

4. Floral Fantasy

Purpose: Flowers can be both fun and relaxing to color, allowing for creativity with color choices.

5. Geometric Journeys

Purpose: Geometric coloring can be particularly absorbing, helping to focus the mind and provide a break from stress.

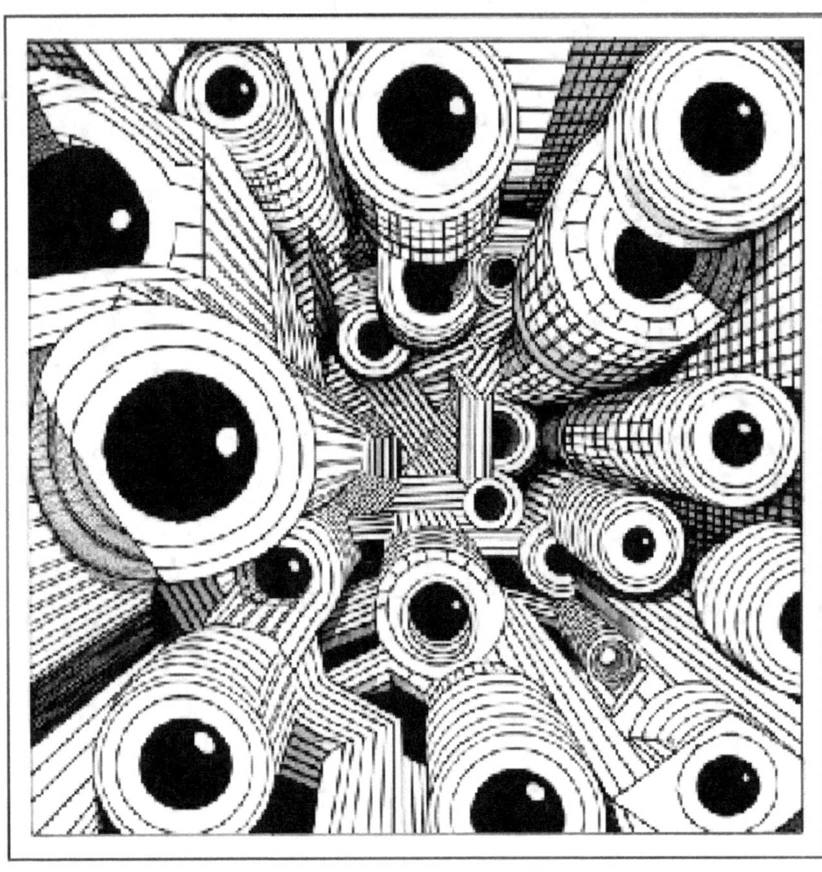

To create these yourself, you can start with simple sketches and then add details as you go. Alternatively, there are many free resources online where you can download and print mindfulness coloring pages. Look for websites that offer free coloring pages for adults, and you'll likely find designs similar to the ones described above. Happy coloring! 🎨✏️

Craft your personalized stress management plan with this template. It helps you outline your stress triggers, the techniques you'll use to tackle them, and your goals. It's like drawing a map to your stress-free destination.

My Stress Plan Template

Welcome to Your Personalized Stress Management Plan!

This template is designed to help you identify your stress triggers, select effective techniques to address them and set clear goals for your stress management journey. Think of it as your roadmap to a more relaxed and balanced life.

PART 1: IDENTIFYING MY STRESS TRIGGERS

1. Trigger #1

- Description
- How it makes me feel
- Times/places it occurs

2 Trigger #2

- Description
- How it makes me feel
- Times/places it occurs

3. Trigger #3

- Description:
- How it makes me feel
- Times/places it occurs

Trigger	Descripti	How it makes	Times/Places it
Trigger			
Trigger			
Trigger			

(Continue as needed)

PART 2: MY STRESS-BUSTING TECHNIQUES

1. Technique for Trigger #1

- Selected Technique
- Why I chose this
- How I plan to implement it

2. Technique for Trigger #2

- Selected Technique
- Why I chose this
- How I plan to implement it

3. Technique for Trigger #3

- Selected Technique
- Why I chose this
- How I plan to implement it

Part 2: My Stress-Busting Techniques

Technique for	Selected	Why I	How I plan to
Technique for			
Technique for			
Technique for			

(Continue as needed)

Part 3: My Stress Management Goals

1. Short-Term Goal #1

- Description
- Steps to achieve it
- Target completion date

2. Short-Term Goal #2

- Description
- Steps to achieve it
- Target completion date

3. Long-Term Goal

- Description
- Steps to achieve it
- Target completion date

Part 3: My Stress Management Goals

Goal Type	Descrip	Steps to	Target
Short-Term			
Short-Term			
Long-Term			

(Continue as needed)

Reflection and Adjustment

Weekly Check-In

- What worked well this week?
- What challenges did I face?
- Adjustments for next week

Reflection and Adjustment: Weekly Check-In

Wee	What Worked	Challenges	Adjustments for
Wee			
Wee			
Wee			
Wee			

(Repeat weekly check-ins and adjust your plan as needed)

FINAL NOTES

- Remember, this is a living document. Adjust and refine it as you learn more about what works best for you.
- Celebrate your progress, no matter how small. Every step forward is a victory in your stress management journey.

Congratulations on taking this important step in managing your stress!

Keep this plan where you can see it and refer to it often. Here's to your journey towards a more peaceful and balanced life!

These worksheets and activities are designed to add a little zest to your stress management practice. They're easy, engaging, and effective - turning the journey to a calmer you into an enjoyable experience. So, grab your pens, pencils, and playful spirit, and let's get cracking on these stress-busting activities!

Your Stress-Busting Support Squad: Where to Find the Pros and Peers

Alright, stress-busting superstars, sometimes even the mightiest of us need a helping hand or a listening ear.

That's where our directory of professional help and support groups comes in - think of it as your go-to guide for finding your stress-busting allies. Whether you're looking for a wise wizard in the form of a therapist or a fellowship of fellow stress-battlers, we've got you covered. Let's dive into where you can find these champions of calm.

Therapists and Counselors: Your Personal Stress Guides

Need someone to help navigate the stormy seas of stress? Therapists and counselors are like lighthouses in the fog. They offer professional guidance, strategies, and a safe space to talk it out. Check out resources like ***Psychology Today*** or local mental health clinics to find a therapist that fits your vibe.

Support Groups: Your Stress-Busting Crew

Sometimes, just knowing you're not alone in the battle can be a huge relief. Support groups offer a space to share experiences, tips, and encouragement. It's like having a team huddle with people who get what you're going through. Websites like ***Meetup*** or local community centers can be great places to start looking for stress management or mental health support groups.

Online Forums: Your Virtual Stress Relief Community

In the digital age, support can also come from the virtual world. Online forums and communities offer a platform to discuss stress management, share stories, and find support from the comfort of your keyboard.

*Platforms like **Reddit,** specific **Facebook** groups, or mental health forums provide a wealth of information and a sense of community.*

Wellness Centers and Retreats: Your Stress Escape Havens

For those who want to combine stress management with a bit of escape, wellness centers and retreats are like mini-vacations for your mind. They offer workshops, activities, and relaxation techniques in a serene setting. It's like hitting the refresh button on your mental state.

Hotlines and Helplines: Your Immediate Stress Lifelines

And let's not forget about hotlines and helplines - these are your immediate go-to resources when you need to talk to someone ASAP. They're like a stress SOS signal, offering immediate support and guidance. Keep a list of these numbers handy, just in case.

This directory is your starting point for finding the right kind of support for your stress management journey. Remember, reaching out for help is a sign of strength, not weakness. So, whether it's professional guidance or a community of support, you're not alone on this journey.

Connect, share, and support each other in our quest for a stress-free life! 🤝 💬 🌐 📞 🧘

About Nora Sage

Nora Sage is a seasoned expert in the realms of stress management and positive psychology. With a warm and engaging approach, she has spent over two decades guiding individuals through the journey of self-discovery and wellness. Nora's passion for helping others find balance and joy in their lives stems from her own experiences as a middle-aged woman navigating the complexities of modern life.

Holding a Master's degree in Positive Psychology, Nora has dedicated her career to exploring the science of happiness and well-being. Her approach is deeply rooted in practical, evidence-based strategies that promote mental resilience and emotional harmony. Nora's expertise lies in transforming life's challenges into opportunities for growth, drawing from a rich tapestry of techniques including mindfulness, cognitive-behavioral therapy, and holistic wellness practices.

As a mother, wife, and professional, Nora understands the delicate art of balancing personal and professional life. Her insights are imbued with empathy and real-world wisdom, making her a relatable and trusted figure in the field of personal development. Through her workshops, books, and personal coaching sessions, Nora has empowered countless individuals to navigate stress with grace and cultivate a life of fulfillment and peace.

Nora's writing style is vibrant and accessible, reflecting her belief that personal growth should be an uplifting and transformative journey. In her latest book, she invites readers to embark on this journey, offering tools and techniques that are both practical and joyous. Nora Sage is not just an author; she's a companion on the path to a more serene and balanced life.

www.ingramcontent.com/pod-product-compliance
Lightning Source LLC
Chambersburg PA
CBHW070848250726

48662CB00003B/1426